OrangeBooks Publication

Smriti Nagar, Bhilai, Chhattisgarh - 490020

Website: **www.orangebooks.in**

© Copyright, 2023, Author

All rights reserved. No part of this book may be reproduced, stored in a retrieval system, or transmitted, in any form by any means, electronic, mechanical, magnetic, optical, chemical, manual, photocopying, recording or otherwise, without the prior written consent of its writer.

Tales Of The Twilight

PRATEEK S KULKARNI

OrangeBooks Publication
www.orangebooks.in

Tales of the Twilight

MICRO TALES

You are the twilight in the night sky,
You are the angel who always outshines,
It is so beautiful that even my words blush in my poems.

In all those lines that I've sent you,
They never made me realize that you fell in love.
And,
I still crave for those teary drops of love to roll down your cheeks
And make this poet blessed to recollect you,
Yet again, in my poems.

If that make out that you imagined was with me,

Then this poet is whistling for the stars to screen the curtain and,

Let's count every candle that storyline our intimacy!

I wonder on my balcony of the clear sky and

A bunch of love showering through beautiful nature.

As the sun rises, the chirps of the birds call for our love and,

I am here writing endlessly for you and about our love.

I pedalled miles to love you,
I found the warmth of love in every mile when I drove towards you.

Lost in the dark,
I lose every inch of mine to remember our love to fade my fear of being in the dark.

I wonder,
How this life craves for you to be mine forever and ever.

He never kept any secrets from her.

Except,

His proposal.

He never framed any sentence by himself.

But, by being lost in her beauty,

He became a poet.

They asked,

Addicted to Love?

Addicted to Her?

No,

Then?

Addicted to 'Her Love', I replied.

Have you cried for somebody? They asked,

Nodding my head,

*'I am still searching for that soul to wipe my tears',
I replied.*

The day you accept me,

It's the rebirth of the joy and happiness that was lost inside me in finding true love.

They wept to be together forever…

But,

They never knew that their tears would make an ocean of love!

He wondered how all broken pieces could be fixed as a heart.

His heart replied,

Only if a part of her still loves a part of him!

You shine bright among all,

You create those sparkling eyes with endless smiles.

I can hear your voice from a distance,

I feel you when you winkle

I said to the star in the sky.

No scar is permanent.

But it turns out to wound if it is for the heart.

I don't miss you,

But I terribly miss 'you' in 'you',

Who once loved me.

You blocked me everywhere,

Yet, every notification feels like yours.

My friend asked me,

What was the best thing that happened to me in the search for happiness?

It started happening when I began writing about her.

- I replied

They have argued, they have fought,
They have shouted, they have cried.
But, more than everything, they loved each other.

He gave up everything for her,
She gave him up for everything.
Mistakes were realized but time was unspoken.

You can choke my heart,
But still, the echoes of my heartbeat would call your name.

What should I have to dedicate to you?

Playlists of songs? or

Mindful of thoughts? or

A heart full of love???

But in the end,

A puzzled state of mine could all say was

'I love you'.

*Love is not when you understand the silence
behind her emotions,*

But,

*It is when you understand her voice behind
the silent tears.*

The empty heart, those loudest cries,

The void chaos, those suffocated breathes,

Never-ending wants, never-ending love,

At last, we count,

Of those little hopes and endless memories.

First time when I cried for you was,
'When I was missing you'.
The last time I cried for you was,
'When I missed you'.

Middle of the night,
Even when those stars are hiding behind,
Making me feel so lonely and
I am wishing for her only sight.
Oh, my beauty, it's the middle of the night,
Unhide yourself, and let's wink at each other.

Those cuddles in your arms,

Warmth filled the space, and we have travelled around the world while kissing each other.

While imagining myself sliding through the rainbow,

I want to be showered by a million stars by holding your hand.

At the end of the fairy tale, I would fall in love all over again.

The evening welcomes her to my paradise;
The golden rays shine on her cheeks and strike my spine to be more romantic.

The cool breeze welcomes the stars and the moon to witness the cosy love story.

You know what?

I still believe you love me,

I still believe I'm your priority,

I still believe you mark me the same as I was to you before,

I still believe you care for me, shout at me, remember me, love me...

Because I still believe you are 'mine'.

*Moon is lonely too, be a light for your stars,
like it makes worth their existence.*

Likely,

*Love is like a coffee bean; you love the essence and taste
the happiness while sipping every memory.*

The time when our skin will be curled and wrinkled,

*Our tears will unfold the memories of our exchanged
love.*

Yet when the world says it's the end of the journey,

*Those captured moments through the lens are the
imprints that we are meant forever.*

You are the blue hope under the grey sky.
I want to hug you to kiss a million stars.
Holding your hand, together we draw a rainbow.
That makes our relationship more colorful than ever.

In a second of anger, he threw the wine bottle.

A broken heart was waiting for her text.
He feels the cuddles in her arms,

Warmth filled the space and they travelled the world while kissing each other.

~He blushed, looking at her photo.

Everyone believed that his heart is a mystery,

And then she proved everyone wrong.

Their little secret was that his heart was just a lock and she was the key.

When I say I love you,
Please believe it is true.

When I say it is forever,
You should know that I will never leave you.

When I say goodbye,
Promise me you won't cry.

Because the day I say so,
Will be the day I will die.

Holding your hand to cross my wish,
I want to feel the gaps between your fingers.

I'll hug you and caress you every time,
Because I love to take care of you.

I will stay with you forever,
In all dusks and dawns.

I will whisper to the moon and stars about us,
Because I want to talk about the purest love story.

You make my life complete.

You laugh with me when I cry, makes me realize you are the purest love.

And, you are mine in my every tear of happiness.

The rising sun called for love.
I replied with morning hugs.
The blue skies appeared to shine with love,
And the sun over my head showered me with the good vibes.

But,
When the sun started to set, little I realized I started to miss you more.
The dark sky appeared to send me your hugs, and the stars witnessed our cosy love.

Hey, you are too pretty!
Want to hang around the city with me?
You are so fancy; you became my fantasy!
Stars are blushing, so my heart is bursting!
Hold my hand, don't crush my heart!

Because we got to rush,
To grab a bite of pizza and sip a coffee under the moonlight where even the stars fall in love!

Don't let tomorrow happen; the rays have turned their ways as a fire.

The morning is not soothing but a nightmare,
The thoughts haunting me every night are now not rare.
These emotions are like mental trauma,
I'm being tortured even without marijuana.

I whisper that everything will be fine,
I know it still cannot match my favourite chime.
I'm scared here, crying in pain,
I'm lonely here, fighting in hell.

You make my heart beat faster.

Just with the mirage of you being here, I shred in happiness.

My arms are craving for your warm hugs.

And this evening cannot wait any longer,

Come here very fast and let's watch the stars together.

This morning was no different; I missed you by my side.

It's been just a couple of hours since I'm awake, but I feel going back to bed.

This weather is making me cosy, but I'm trying harder not to be in bed.

I'm hugging a pillow but rather I wish you were here.

Come here soon, let's enjoy the rain, feel the chills, and let's cuddle with kisses until we fall asleep together.

Tales of the Twilight

Is something missing?

Maybe your hugs, maybe be your kisses,

Oh, it's a long day!

I missed you every while; I missed you around the clock.

But here are my hugs and kisses for the night, we want to share, the memories that we want to create.

Let me watch the golden skyline and enjoy the sun setting behind the horizon that says today's love was amazing.

Before twilight, I want to write in my diary of the first kiss of warm sunshine and the chirps of the birds,

The melody of those made me feel dancing with you to our favourite song.

Let tomorrow's sunshine be bright as same, and with my warm hugs from this end.

I'll hug you hard until there is no space between.

This poet is twining the words to describe how the eyes were locked.

Little do you understand, before this poet writes the next line, pull him closer and kiss until he makes you smile.

I want to count the stars and fall asleep,

On those counts, I want to remember how much you mean to me.

This universe is irreplaceable, lucky I've found you.

By looking at those stars, I want to sleep on your lap, I want to listen to your lullabies.

The words of your love are my favourite language of expression, hold my hand and let's count those stars together.

Want to hold your waist and dance to our favourite music.
I will hold your hand and make you swirl like a butterfly,

I look at your pretty eyes and hear my heartbeat,
There is a silence around, but it's only us and this music,

Nothing can stop us from being explorers,
And this hug is the moment to capture.

You are the storm; you are the peace.

You are the whisper; you are the mighty bomb.

You are the cuddle; you are the gentle touch.

You are the soft mist; you are the roaring void.

You hide the love under the rainbow,

You are the string of love vibrating the clear sky.

*Like the moon whispers and the stars glitter,
I write those love stories and witness the cosy warm hugs.*

At least in this poem, I write about the rainbow and that curve in your smile, which makes this writer to fall in love.

Amidst the bright stars, I stayed in the dark.

Little I want is to shine and smile.

A little more to laugh and love.

But to be alone in this beautiful sky is a chaos.

Hold me for a while, love me a little more.

I can be the poet and make my every poem to sing stories for you.

Tales of the Twilight

I failed every time to ask for a hug.
Again, this time,
I really don't know how to ask,
This writer is out of words.
I am talking to the dark sky about the stars.
And in this dark world, I genuinely wait for the million hugs.

Striving for love,
He found her beneath the struggles.
He found his happiness beneath their love.
He found the melody tuning his throat.
His life was like a roller coaster ride,
Swinging through life and penning everything his heartbeat has cried in melancholy!

*It's almost sunset; waves are kissing beneath the foot;
Tickles are stronger than the tides.*

*Little you raise your chin and look into my eyes,
Let's hold onto each other and kiss until even those stars feel jealous.*

*Can I look into your eyes for one more time?
To tell the world how beautiful they sparkle while they speak of million expressions.*

Under the million shades of twilight,
I want to hold your waist and dance to the melodies of
those stars and the moon.

Your curve is like an hourglass that chills my veins.
The knot of our ecstasy and love bites to the infinite.
The night was the truth which only we knew.

That was when,
Even the stars blushed at how beautifully our love is
drawn.

The stars glitter all over like the horizon.
They spread the love like the whole atmosphere.
I wandered on my balcony of its love and the vibes.
It was then I thought of you to whisper the love,
I missed you by my side to be cuddled until dawn.

When it is a new beginning, there is a smile;
The smile of new hopes and happiness.

Out of all the blues, I found the rainbow.
Its colours are majestic
When I think of you,
Butterflies tickle all over.

Is there no escape?
Because I feel like I am hugged tight in your arms.

It is all dark here,
Dark I mean, the way stars wink at me and the moon loves me.

This poem is speaking of our love and the way we have rolled.

There is hope in every dark,
Because our love always brings light to my poems.

I wish you were right next to that window,
If you were, every day and night, I would peek at you and never miss the serenity.
In my every beautiful dream, you stand out to be my hope.
I wish someday we make ourselves a home.

When the clouds are dark and the rain brings scars,
Tell me, where is the peace?

Clogged heart and suffocated breaths,
Atleast tell me, where is the sunshine?

Days are gone and nights are wild;

The sweats of heavy breaths are turned as the tone of sacred dried throat,
The tears are overloaded and the shivers are restless,
This dark is terrible, like the clogged heart unable to think of happiness.

When the dark is cold and you fall in love with the way it chills your spine.
Remembrance of your love is just a reason to smile.

The truth is you want to shiver endlessly.
But only if it is for ecstasy.

A part of me wants to KISS YOU.
But, have I ever really told you how much I MISS YOU?

Oh, it's a shame of love, which is a tragedy!
But I won't lie because ours is a beautiful LOVESTORY.

May these stars shower you the bliss and sparkle to wink, because that's the way I KISS.

POEMS

When you see a star,
You never dream to shine bright like her,
You never feel left alone,
You never feel hatred,
You never wish to travel to her.

But seeing a star,
You feel the soul within you,
You feel you are gifted,
You feel you are loved,
You just wish she is always yours.

After all the above, when you,
Dedicate lines to her,
Write poems on her,
Compose songs on her,
It is when you hear your heartbeat.

And that is when you whisper, 'I love you'.

Today when I go back to my sleep,
I'm going to share your love with my pillow.
Will say the way we spent the day,
The way our hearts have met and our eyes were locked.

Your cuteness in your voice,
Crushed my heart in all the possible ways.
Your every melody has sung your beautiful stories,
Yet, made me lost in tuning my love story.

All my dreams were true,
Where I was lost in my poems.
Poems that I've written for you and for our love.
Today,
It's the proof to say that we are together and forever!

Out of everything I've lost,
I found you.
Out of everything I have,
I lost myself within you.

Love has no fate.
It is like the morning sunrays and moonlight at night.

It just showers the bright charms
by abiding the purest love.
It just glooms in the skyline,
By sending stars to love me back!

Secrets are aloof, never heard...
Tears are sacrificed, never cried...
I am ripped, never hugged...

This soul is cornered, suffocating every while,
This soul is drenched, cold and intoxicated,
This soul is dark, hoping for the light.

All my wounds speak of how broke I am.
All my dreams at night have never happened right.
When all my charms were spitted out, it was when I
realised how I am burnt being alive.

Be my side forever!

Be my side to laugh with me,
Be my side to wipe my tears
Be my side to pat my back when I'm low,
Be my side to share my success,
Be my side to hug me when I need it,
Be my side to kiss me when I get high,
Be my side to conquer the world.

But without you,
I have nothing to be happy about and to enjoy life.
Little you understand, I feel void without you being my side.

Glancing at my old memories,
Black & white photos are still colourful in my heart,
Replenishing the old talks and endless chats.

Sun is dawn, stars are on the horizon.
Every skyline is our hope and belief.
I am far away and craving for togetherness.

Oceans are loud, waves are high.
I am on the shore, being left so alone.
Want to be a free bird, want to be heard.

Ceasing into old times, holding a beer.
Yet so sober, cornered myself closer.
My voice is unheard, love is unfeared.

Those black & white photos are still only a memory,
For me, it's a glory,
To find myself not so lonely.

*There was a time, I was frozen into,
My love was sacred, where you left.*

*We had no reason to fall in love,
Our ship was sunk in the middle of the ocean.*

The wind casting the direction, directed towards the false hope. I am still here, waiting for the truth.

*I am flying over the waves, reaching out so far.
Upon the endless waves, I want to witness our one last kiss.*

Maybe this day will never end,
Maybe tomorrow would never happen,

Maybe this time is very unreal,
Maybe these people never existed.

Maybe everything is an illusion,
Maybe everything is so real.

Maybe I should hug myself to understand that everything is happening real,
Happening right here, right now.
Or,
Maybe I should ask you for a hug right now?

Is it you? Or is it me?
Is it us? Or is it our love?

Craved for happiness, shredded for a surprise!
Smiled at the faults, laughed at the mistakes!

Hugged to wipe the tears,
Kissed to feel our warmth,
Locked by promises,
Cemented by wishes.

Hoped for togetherness,
Believed in love,
Tattooed for the new beginning,
Pierced for the new journey.

Is it you? Or is it me?
Is it us? Or is it our love?
Still left behind,
Behind our unexpressed feelings, unconfessed stories
and untold fate.

This soul wants to snore…
But,
In all the sleepless nights, it just cried while
remembering those nights of flaws and felt a heavy
heart!

Broken soul, irresistible to join!
Shattered heart, unable to shape!
Ripped throat, impossible to laugh!

When he was a kid, he was the most generous soul of an
innocent voice laughing aloud like a hidden melody!

When today,
When he turns himself in this chaotic world,
The world which has made to disappear his self-love,
It has made to forget his charms,
It has made to realise that he is not in his own arms!

Every time I miss you, baby, in my arms,
It reminds me, how much I miss us.

All those letters reached an empty reply,
Still, an empty heart of mine, waited for your love.

Every morning it reminds me of writing a letter filled with hopes.
For all those, didn't mattered to you in anyway.

Tell me now or write for me now.
I know that your bin is filled with my love.

Out of aloud, I'm like a shattered piece.
Like a lonely soul drenched in rain.

I am here for you darling, still writing to you every day.
I still hope that I will receive your letter one day.

Every day I hope you write for me too, and love for us will make its way,
Those letters will hug us in love and make us a happy one.

I can watch our photos whole day!

Our crazy talks and when our eyes met,
Thanks to the photographer for the candid!
Those candid speak of our emotion and love which marks how deep is our love!

It was when I hugged you,
Old memories were recollected.
It was when our eyes met,
I felt the love and hope of togetherness.

Thanks to all the good times,
I wish we can be together forever.
And nevertheless,
Let's create an ocean of love and memories.

When everything was new,
You made me familiar with everything.
When everyone was new,
You were my dearest.

In finding the real ones,
I found the true soul.
When everything was dark,
You were my light.

When I was hopeless,
You just hugged me and whispered, you are 'mine'.
Those lines of yours still make me miss you.

Missing you,
Makes me feel, I am losing everything again.
Makes me find everyone stranger again.
Makes me feel, I am losing myself.
Makes me feel, you are putting me into dark cage.

Now,
Can I please hug you and whisper, you are still 'mine'?

Should I walk miles? Or
Should I count my steps?

For every step collecting my tears,
Like sailing without the oars, I am unable to find my destiny.

With the vibes of morning rise, my thoughts on you build up.

Your never-ending hugs, kisses and unconditional love,
And our relationship beyond those emotions.

All our faults looked like tiny stars but,
Our love covered everything like warm blue skies.

But my fear of losing you raised when sun was setting,
Only stars started appearing in the skies.

Little I understood all those stars outdid the skyline and
I=n the same way our faults set our relationship.

When I remember you,
Tears will roll down my cheeks.
When my eyes cry for you,
My heart cries for our love.

When my own shadows do not follow me,
Then I understand you are too busy to remember me.

But,
When we found ourselves drifting apart,
I still chose to be loved in your arms.
When my hopes were shattered,
I trusted our love would still find its way.

But now,
When I remember you,
My tears will tell our tale.
When my eyes cry for you,
My heart still beats for our love.

When my own shadows aren't following me,
I illusion you holding my hand.
When the days turn to nights,
I want the stars to tell our love story.

Even if my hopes are shattered,
I still believe we are destined to be 'together'.

I love dreams!
I want my dreams to talk to me.
I want to design the beautiful memories.

I want her to be with me in the warmth dreamland where it welcomes only us to the most beautiful space.

I again, mention I and only her!
But,

I still am not able to find 'her',
For whom I am addressing as the most beautiful angel of my dreamland.

You are my love; You are my warmth.
You are my secret; You are my hope.
You are my laugh; You are my silence.
You are my pain; You are my healing.
You are my strength; You are my weakness.

Just wanna hug you, to feel your heartbeat.
Just wanna hug you, to feel comfort.
Just wanna hug you, to erase all my pain.
Just wanna hug you, to share secrets.
Just wanna hug you, to make you mine.

Hold my hand in this beautiful world,
Hug me in this chaotic world,
Just whisper to me, 'I love you',

We will,
Jump off together for every laugh and pain of our lives.

I write when I laugh,
I write when you cry;

I write when I cry,
I write when you laugh;

There is a little exchange! Oh dear,
Did I just forget to mention 'our love'?

Yes, it is our laughs and cries that echoes for our love.
Please take me back to that world.

To the world,
Where you left me unsaid,
But I heard your whispers.
Where you left me hated,
But I hugged your love.

Little I have understood,
When I write, it is for our love that my pen wishes to write.
When I write, it is our journey that my paper defines our love.

I was a lone kid, wandering about blue skies,
Made me realise, the rainbow is beautiful.

I was a lone kid, wandering about the thunderstorms,
Made me realise, how your silence was much louder.

I was a lone kid, wandering through the stars,
Made me realise, even my love can shine once in
lifetime.

I was a lone kid, wandering how this soul could ever find
one has made me realise, my life has twists and turns
too.

And now, when I look back,
I can see the memories of us left behind.
Not the ashes but the glitters of millions of emotions.

My arms have missed you so much,
You have been away the whole time,
My eyes have cried so much,
My heart has felt so much.

Oh! It's a love, it's a love, oh! It's a love...

Your smile makes me happy,
Your hug makes me complete,
Your touch dazes me every time,
We forget the world while we dance.

Oh! It's a love, it's a love, oh! It's a love...

It's our anniversary; oh! I remember,
It's always a new start; oh! We love that,
Let's mark the date,
Let's frame this moment of togetherness.

Oh! It's a love, it's a love, oh! It's a love...

When, every time I fall for her, my heart cries for her!
When, every time I cry for her, my tears will have our love!
When, every time I write for her, even the stars get jealous!

When everything was clear, we dreamt of unvanishing love!
When everything was clear, we held our hands to the world!
When everything was clear, ocean made its way to reflect even the stars!

When those oceans were swept away,
My reasons to love you, still unanswered.
Our reasons to love us, still unfaded.
For your reasons to leave me behind, I'm still a lost kid!

Come back again, like when my heart cried for you!
Come back again, like my tears felt with love!
Come back again, as those stars are still jealous!

*My shaking hands took three tries to light my cigar.
I tried for three million times to forget you, yet failed, I realised how numb I was!*

*I remember everything from our first kiss to the last goodbye,
My corner bed can still smell the letters that I am writing for my love even today,
I realised how much I love you!*

*When every time you smiled,
I remember how our love happened even when my camera blushed more than me!*

*Though the destiny was unknown,
Those lenses were the imprints that we are meant to be forever.*

*Those morning chirps under the blue skies, holding your hand in that beautiful place.
It was like the shades of a rainbow witnessing the love and spreading the happiness.*

*Come dance with me now by holding my hand.
I will grab your waist to kiss intensely,
Last night's petrichor is the truth for our endless love!*

I guess, it's the beginning, I can feel the breeze of happiness.
The vibes of a colourful rainbow and the aesthetic dots of stars that makes this writer to start his story.

There were days of loneliness, but I guess not anymore,
Because there is hope and I believe in us.

For us, it is a platter of ceremony and we should understand we share a great bond.
Something like this had never happened before.
But, it's not strange because I've fallen in love with you long ago.

But somewhere we had confessed ourselves, but were never outspoke.
I know silence was a barrier otherwise, memories had gotten more bundles.
But as they say, it's never the late, I believe the sprout of this journey be sweet and hang onto each other.

I'm stuck here... Thinking about you... Of the lines, I want to dedicate to you, of the love I want to recompose. How can I ask you for a hug? For the kisses? For the warmth this body needs, may-be for one last time before this soul departs.

Maybe tomorrow you ask for the thin stardust about how much I loved you.
Or maybe to the star in the black serene, honestly, she knows me the best.

After I am gone, talk to the memories if I have left anything.

Because when I was there with you, I tried everything to make you laugh and love.
To those dusts of mine, can you please hold in your palms? Because I want to feel the gaps between your fingers for one last time.

In this deepest divine of the purest love,
I found the meaning of eternity.

Sometimes as loud as an ocean and peaceful as a glittering star,
I gaze at the moon and I become perplexed.

May-be because you are beautiful as the moon and stars,
or maybe you make my poem more romantic.

But little did I know I'd become apocalypse when I realised, we are so close yet too far.

A mighty fall, stars glittering all over.
I looked up and said, 'This night is beautiful'.

Like a fairy dream of a little boy who meets his angel,
I watched you near the camp fire.

Your eyes spoke of thunders, and my spine shivered,
I was traumatised when my words trembled.

The cool breeze rippled my shirt, and this deep midnight caught you at my first sight,

I wrapped you in my arms, our hugs made us a little closer and the love filled all those spaces.

I feel something incomplete, bewildered to find myself in this favourite music of yours's,

But little you understand, we both fell in love under this dark sky watching those stars together.

I am here with you forever, to love you forever.
Don't be so low because you know that this love is infinite... Don't be so low.

I write about you in my words, of this love that we have held over years.
You please understand I am here alone.
Writing in every dusk, every dawn.

In my poems, those jingles call you every time.
My heart cries in pain for the love every time.
The words I've inked and expressed every time.

For the things that matter to me, I know you've always cared.
For the love, this soul had decided even to meet the shooting stars.
I am just here under the moonlight, craving for undying love.

Eyes are red,
Sleep is forgotten,
Dreams are shattered,
Loved is faded.

Feelings are muted,
Heart is broken,
Laughs are void,
Mascara is smudged all over.

Hugs are just in memories,
Kisses are sacred in pockets,
Cuddles are just mirages,
Our numbers are dialled for never.

The love abided in our hearts still echoes for a 'need',
The silent distanced hearts cry for 'wants',
The long drives are braked like on a deserted island,
The breaths are shivering every while.

*Crossing the fingers for one phone call or at least a text.
My heartbeat raced to cement this distanced relationship.*

*Yet feeling the insecurities, it was hard but,
Convinced to my love that you have a second chance.*

*Are my poems remembering you or our memories?
Are my words calling for you or the promises?
Is my voice thriving for you or for our warm love?
Does everything of mine is crying for you or for the love to happen again?*

Little do I know; I am calling for you again!!!

Like the stars are never counted but the beauty is always admired.
Like the rainbow is never traced but the colours are drawn so beautifully,
Like the love can never be explained but it has to be felt.

There was a lone poet,

Writing about the dark sky ravished with the shiny glitters.
Painting the colours of rainbow like his life has happened.
This poet has never been in love but his words became a silent message to make others love a beautiful story.

You remind me of the love lines,
You make me say those magical words.

There is much dark here,
Give me some light and lead me forward.

This soul is shivering,
Warm me with your love.

Hold my hand and hug me hard,
Make me smile for one last time.

Take me back to the time,
I want to lose myself in your arms.

I can feel your touch even at a distance,
Even this silence has spoken about love in its own way.

The dark has been covered for an empty reason,
Ocean is beyond my eyesight; so is my love.

I can swim across to hug you once again,
I can hear our favourite song that gives me hope you are somewhere nearby.

Its melodies remind me of when we had danced together,
Memories of every move that made us to fall in love.

The morning hues and blues.
I want to spend my day with you to play the cues.

I am hugged in your arms as this air has wrapped me,
I am wondering what's left, because happiness is filled inside me.

To a fresh start and new beginning,
You have given me flying wings.

To talk about the love, oh, look at your eyes; they are shining bright.
I know I am blushing, but I have hope for this new beginning.

*The haze and the golden-brown skies, and its
lushful breeze in the evening escapes.*

*Your eyes are sparkling, and our love is hiding.
Not to fade but to blush for our symphony.*

*It's been quite a while since I have kept quiet,
Little I thought to write this poem for you.*

*Please uncover before dawn,
Please read aloud to the stars that glitter in the night
sky.*

*Wave with your kisses because I am winking back.
Let's whisper our love and capture our moment
Before this poem is read aloud.*

Like the moon and like the stars,
Are the happiness and the sorrows.
Have you ever felt like listening to their stories?

Like the lush green here and like the whipped blue there,
Are the struggles and the dreams.
Have you ever felt like experiencing it?

Like the tears and like the smiles,
Is the person and the person in you.
Have you ever felt like talking to him/her?

It's the life vs the living,
Have you ever felt to ask the difference?

I want to go out in rain and feel the drops kissing my cheeks.

Tap the rain with endless stories of my scars and cry aloud to say to the world, where I whispered melancholically.

To all the silent despairs enchanted as strong bolds in life,
Holding your hand and grabbing your waist, I was intensified!

Pulling you closer to me and rolling my hands to caress your hair while I whispered you are mine.

Unable to cry, cannot withstand the pain.
Sorry, this is too much for me, for my love, it didn't ask because it's pure.

Poor fellow wandered the blue sky,
But it turned grey with a thunder.

I am standing on the balcony wiping my tears,
Of those drops of rain could also feel my pain.

All I wish for is your hugs and kisses,
I know I will treasure this moment forever if it's cherished along with you.

When you are here, I will have my happiness.

The time goes on and off, but you be my constant.

I know I compare love to the moon and stars and you can ask me, even if they are constant.

But little I want you to know that I compared you with them because they are the rarest!

When the wind blows, I can feel your hug.

Of which is very special so it should be treasured.

I know we have spent quite a time and we should also know that there is a lot more.

Abiding in each other's ups n downs, let's hang onto each other forever!

*The cry of the love is beautiful.
The chirps of the bird in the morning and the violet hues spread across the sky in the dawn.*

*When you write letters to the moon and stars,
There are tiny glitters shining on your cheeks under the vanity lights.*

You capture the lush green view from the balcony on your favourite trip, happiness when you walk in the subway and the stranger smiles.

Wishing to be loved while holding the sky lanterns before you release into the dark sky. How beautiful the love portrays itself!

Take me back to the place where I belong.

Not in the chaos, not in the rush.

But, to the place where everything turns to permanent silence.

Let this mind untwine and the heart loses its relations and may this soul be free.

The suffering of yesterdays and the unhealthy thoughts of today,

Atleast don't let my tomorrows be painful.

End this drama, this story, and I am happy if you take me back to the place where I belong.

When you cited, I am taller & you feel protected when you hug me.
I replied,
It is not that you are shorter nor I am tall, it is your elevation which is cute.

But, little you understand,
That hug will always be filled with millions of trusts, promises and love!

When you mentioned that my shoulders are broad and muscular that you can rest on them forever,
I replied you with a silent thanks!

But, little do you understand,
You can rest on it whenever you feel low, sad or depressed and note that they are just for you to pillow share your feelings.

Standing on my balcony,
Watching the raindrops racing to kiss the land.
Holding a mug of coffee and smelling the petrichor,
Remembering you and our love,
Talking over the phone and exchanging kisses.

When the rain has stopped and still,

Standing on my balcony,
But now, land has slowly started drying up after the rain,
Coffee mug is empty and sun raising,
Little did I realise how our love faded,
Checking the empty call dials, my tears rolled down.

Little do you understand,
I am still standing on my balcony, holding the coffee mug and,
Waiting for the call and for our intimacy.

POETRY

Jingles were heard melodious, waves were hitting the shore, fingers were locked, hands were crossed into each other's and we walked a mile. Little we knew water was tickling under the feet and happiness was found beneath. Its past twilight and I wanted to save everything for tonight. Like the chaos away from the crowd but like the peace amidst the woods. Like the loud grey pastel over the horizon, but like the palettes of rainbow dancing off the clouds. This beauty is so soothing; I feel blessed and loved. And yes, thank you for holding my hand.

When I look into your eyes, it speaks thousands of words and draws millions of emotions. I feel traumatised to pull you closer and whisper, 'I love you'. But I pushed myself not to. Can I hug you one more time to make myself smile? Also, I am falling in love within no time. Let us climb the mountain and at the peak, hope we find ourselves. And in that journey, let's not forget our cute little dramas that made each other feel special. I don't know about tomorrow, but today, I want to fall into your arms and feel the warm cuddles. Let's fall in love and kiss each other until the curtains are drawn in shyness. I don't know about tomorrow, but today, until my last breath, I promise that I will make you feel special because you are always mine.

Can you be that star every poet wishes to write upon? In the night with the cosy jingles and red wine with a melodious music to make my words dance to the love that I imagine every time.

Yes, I remember my last night when I was writing poetry. After twilight, when the sun was setting behind the clouds and the dark space vanished above my head. It was when I drew the sparkles and imagined a celestial was jotted to call me to fall in love. How beautiful, right? When the years are spent without anyone holding my hand and where the echoes of my pain were louder than the thunders, I closed the curtain from the outside world. In the dark-covered space of my world, I saw a moonlight writing an invitation to join a party with the events of my life.

Holding my pen to write about my life, I remembered my red eyes, dried lips, black circles, pale smile and clumsy hair with a tired soul. I started writing about love and romance of my love had never seen nor experienced. But my every write-ups was a secret message by those stars. Stars, became the lifeline of my every emotion to the outside world.

Prateek S Kulkarni

This soul is finding the light clearing its every shadow and hoping it to be a mirage. And to the world, this writer just wants to hug and embark even on his every little happiness.

~

I am sitting on my balcony by reading our old conversations. I am sitting on my balcony and rewinding the days and nights that I had spent all by myself. Today, I sipped a coffee with a strong brewed caffeine of your love and started my day. Before the coffee was sipped, I looked at you and said, 'Hey beautiful'. The reply showed up and I was ready to start my day. Yes, I want to tell you about myself. I want to tell you about myself a lot but in short. You may find a reason for me to act stupid. But I have a reason to be explicit. I want to take your short time to say how much I love you. The three words mean three milestones of happiness. The sweetness of sugar, the vibrance of the rainbow, the beauty of a feather; they mix my emotions to make my love for you and my happiness as no separation. This heart beats for togetherness and the desires burn deep within to share my life with you to join the dots and make us the perfect one. I know you are wondering about my point to write this for you. And yes, I just started liking you at every dusk and down. The melancholy of this evening is filled with the cool breeze and tangling this guitarist to play the love story. His string vibrates the harmony that I crave for the stars during the candle light dinner.

In the echoes of the waves hitting the shores every time, I found the love in your eyes when the first time I felt I was losing myself. I felt my heart was beating faster. Shifting to the world of melancholy, you became my favourite jingle bell. The aura of our sweet conversation made my nerves to see you badly and the gaps of my fingers wanted to be fitted by yours.

I never believed that magic would bring happiness until I felt you. I never believed that magic would be like the stars that shines and the moon that showers the love. I never failed to write so beautifully thinking about you. Even in the darkest of nights, you become to appear as my full moon. This cosy cool breeze ripping through my shirt wants to hug you. When you called me during the dawn, I never knew I could fall for your voice and love you beyond until the beautiful sunset.

The strings of my guitar want to sing for you and my camera wants to capture your smile every time. But I want you to know, undoubtedly, my pen wants to write our love and, I hope you understand 'I love you'.

Hold my hand for once; I will promise that I will protect you forever. Make this relationship a meaningful journey and find the meaning for eternal escapes.

Love is always loved, hated, cried, shouted, wept and lost. But, love never fails to say, 'I love you'.

Walk with me in the night. Let's count the stars together. Hug me when I shiver. Let your skin brush to mine and the moon says its fine. In our kisses, let our heart beats faster and the spaces of our fingers fill with the warm jingles. Let's dance together to the rhythm and when you look at me to send me the whisper of love, my spine shivers to numb.

I cry every night; I laugh every day; I cry every day and I laugh every night knowing the reality that you cannot be mine. I lock myself to cry in the corner of my room to let you never know how I am left alone.

When you ask me, 'Any poems for today?
It makes me think of 'yesterday'.

Yesterday when she was with me,
Yesterday when she gave me those joyful memories,
Yesterday when I was her priority,
Yesterday when she had promised to stay forever.

When you ask me, 'Any poems for today?
It makes me think of 'today'.

Today where I still hope she is with me,
Today I still find my happiness in those memories,
Today it's not the priorities that matter to her,
Today she never even remembers her promise.

When you ask me, 'Any poems for today?
It makes me think of 'tomorrow'.

Tomorrow where I will be left alone,
Tomorrow where I get scared of being rejected,
Tomorrow where my dreams would be shattered,
Tomorrow where I would be jealous of seeing you with someone else.
This is all because I still 'love you'.

Those little cries,
It still echoes of a little kid, unaware of herself lost in her own little world, when she was five.

Those little cries,
It still echoes of a little kid, chanting to know herself, lost in people's judgement, when she was ten.

Those little cries,
It still echoes of a little kid, finding herself lost in her own space, when she was fifteen.

Those little cries,
It still echoes of a little kid, fighting for her freedom lost in a chaotic world craving for her skin, when she was twenty.

Those little cries,
Have now turned into loud cries, withholding her scars and wounds, unaware of the secret lust surrounding her.

The little kid is raped.
Yes, she has blood stains,
Used by those she herself trusted as family.

Prateek S Kulkarni

She is lost, unable to find herself.
After all, those chants ended her in most disrupted ways.
This world has become so inhuman.

She is lost with no abiding love.
For the love, she wished a happy life.
This world has left only the blood stains on her.

She is lost, searching for the purest love.
For her love, people judged by her scars.
This world has left her no life.

While traveling on a train,

I am standing near the door...

Exposing my half-body to fly in the air.

The cool breeze and the edge of my stance made my heartbeat heavier.

Honks of this train n bogie's vibration to wheel sets,

Started setting my happiness into a corner!

Seeing the red signal at distance reminded me of my isolation.

And now, I put my half-head outside my platform,

Waving a hand to the co-passenger from another compartment.

Finding the stranger more passive and shrugged myself in despair.

Hey, myself, how about a jump?

From this pace of running train?

Jump to make people understand that I faced world of loneliness?

Hey, myself, looking at my leg waving half opened into the air.

The pendulum made me realize how ambulatory my life was.

Looking back to my old days, like my leg has walked across the borders.

It just reminded me of how my love was whispered in other beings.

Yes, when my pendulum stopped, I realised I was so tired.

Tired in search of love in others after walking miles.

And still standing near the door, waiting for my destination.

Destination to get down, to step into that world waiting genuinely for pure love.

Where all my dramas and traumas of chaotic life will find an end.

Where I start my new journey of love with you and start writing the poetries just for you!

Life is like a poetry. The imagination beyond flying in space when happiness filled like the touch of cloud nine. Sadness flowing like being as a hopeless down in the dumps. But the surprises of goosebumps when you stand in front of your loved ones. Also, poetry is like the excitement when you are shaking hands with the angel of your dreams. The regret you talk about refusing the dozens of proposals while you were following your dreams. The desire burning into my words expresses that I want to feel her and touch the soul love like a baffle.

But all of a sudden, an instant of my future says, you are counting your last breaths. Then I realised I have never given a damn about my present. Life is like a see-saw, up and down, unbalanced with the past and the future, but my pendulum never rested in present. I want to be the man of billion dreams filled with hopes and desires; I want to be the man who never stops spreading happiness to find love and sacrifices in my yesterdays.

Now, I am standing on my balcony and counting the stars while the music is playing in the recorder. I opened the last bottle of alcohol while I lighted the cigar. A shooting star is just whistling in my vision. I am traumatized, lost in the spirit of alcohol, unable to withstand the happiness after seeing my love. Just right there, right in front of my eyes, I stepped to move forward with every second I felt she is fading away. Love hugged me after 28 years of wait. The journey was all alone without you. The empty heartbeats and the shiver of lub-dub, lub-dub for 28 years have never given me a single pause to hope for my love.

After tonight, when I am gone, I still believe this soul had its last wish. Please discover, please read, please feel the love I have written in my poetries. Those poetries will speak of my lonely heartbeat and tears scenting like hopes and dreams of my desires. Make this lover a beautiful memory and keep it in the book of secrets, I promise I can hold the thorns if you let me discover even a peck of happiness in our love for one last time. All I waited is for your single text or at least a wave of final goodbye when at least I took my last breath.

Hello love, tonight you stand on my balcony and I will give you thousands of kisses while you experience the shooting star that reminds me of my yesterday.

There is this something in my mind, it's been a while, but rather to melt like an ice, the thoughts are piling every now and then,

Have you ever been in a state where you are in a trance of billion thoughts racing inside, but only the tears of agony reply to the situation? It is not easy, it's like a lemon is squeezed until the last drop. It's fine; it was completely fine to some point. But I never realised, the squeeze was into a fresh milk. How funny life takes turns.

I am here, the clock striking at 2 am in the morning. I am still not decided what to write about. But this midnight has only given me the cool breeze with the memories of shattered pasts, unvalued love and choking pain. But, this silence around is not easy to hug, it's all only the pain that I have to accept.

But this time, I am writing about the silence that is hugging me uncomfortably; When I lost my first love, it was like a shadow where I never felt the pain leaving my side. Like a mirage where I never felt like she is coming back. Like a speck of dust that is disappeared into thin air.

Prateek S Kulkarni

For the world I can scream aloud and say I want you, I want to revisit those days where my heart was felt, my happiness was into light and my love was fulfilled. But today, I am still sober even after consuming every bottle of alcohol from the case. These jingles aren't soothing anymore, my body just wants to hear your whispers. Cigars are burning me inside, hands are shaking without you in my arm, kiss me until my heart can sing along. This distance is really suffocating and I know I can just talk only with the stars. Because I know at the end of the day it's the memories of us that will give me a reason to breathe and wait until you come back and whisper, 'You are mine'.

I woke up one morning and found a part of me was paralyzed. I felt broken and cried inside by seeing you not there at my side. I wish yesterday's thunders were heard because the silence of this morning was much louder. I was heartbroken with a heavy heart, choking breathes and weeping in the corner of my bed.

I had to move out of my bed. Kicked myself without a ray of happiness. Headed to the kitchen to make some breakfast. But I missed your hugs from behind like you used to wrap me in your arms while I chop tomatoes and toss omelette every time. Now, the omelette on the table is not delicious and the coffee is not strong enough for me to move on.

Even this warm sunshine feels so much grey because I am numb to accept that you have left me all alone in the beautiful frame. My shirt still smells of your perfume that had been shared in our hugs and cuddles every time. My arms want to wrap around your waist, my eyes want to capture your smile, my lips want to feel your kisses and what-not? You must also know that wherever you have gone, you have left me like a dead living inside.

I guess I need to pause here thinking of why you even disappeared after our last night love. I guess instead I need to shout aloud to this world to make it understand that I am coming for you, to meet my love, to hug you once again by wrapping my arms around your waist. I will kiss you to say this soul needs you.

Of all the good and bad we have shared, I never wanted us to end in this way.

And when one fine day, I finally received your letter and you said;

"Sorry I didn't leave a message nor ever tried to contact you. I know it's been a couple of years in our lives. I want to say that time has passed but not my love. Before I write this letter, I don't want you to ask me why I didn't leave you any message the other day."

But all I can say is these couple of years were hard as it were for you too. Every day I remembered you, every day I cried for you, every day I loved you and missed being in your arms. I missed the times when you understood my silence; you were my alarm with a great brewed coffee. I am just one call away. Let's hang out and revisit our old dramas and once again fall into each other's arms to watch the sunset. Let's chime the wine glass and watch the buttery flashback of every moment we had lived for ourselves and for our future. Future, where we had pictured us in a beautiful frame.

~

12

Sssshhhh!!! Please leave me alone. Yes, I am crying, pouring my tears for almost an hour now. Can you please let it flow? At least after this time, I want to smile, I want to laugh again and when I cry, my tears hold my scars; my scars speak of my pain. The pain of loneliness. and loneliness when I am alone! Being left alone is a next big thing, big thing to me since ages. Sssshhhh!!!

I am wiping my tears. No wait, was I really supposed to cry? Cry at this hour? Will my pain be gone? Will my memories be erased? Can I smile now? Can I be able to? or something like this will ever happen again? Why can I sense the worse is hitting me in some time again? Is this normal? Am I normal? Or will this happen to everyone? Or am I the only one?

Sssshhhh!!! Depression is the next big thing and I am already onto it. Can somebody explain why this beautiful blue sky is looking like a scary mirage? Why does the musical chirps of these birds hear like raspy croaks? Why does the vibrant colours of a rainbow look pale and dull? I am here, the waves are hitting the shore and this isn't interesting to me anymore. Why aren't the stars and moon talking to me like the way they were talking before? Are these the signs of the depression to sulk me even more?

Okay, tell me now, give me at least a hope that when after I finish weeping from the corner of my bed, everything will be okay.

But I am not sure this isn't the last time I would cry. I am already seeing myself in that corner of my bed suffocating between the pillows; Pillow? Yeah, they are my best buddies and at least they listen to my stories. It's dark now and I guess I need to check my moon and stars. To my pillow listening to my whole night, it's time for me to go. Sun is above my head and I need to start the struggles of my day. See you at night, until then I miss you.

When I saw you sitting on the balcony all alone by yourself, I am really sorry, I was hurt too, in a flick of next second, it made me realise of those days when we were together. Do you even know that balcony has heard millions of our stories while sipping the hot brewed coffee and has seen the thousands of pictures of us while we cuddled to sleep in each other's arms while looking at stars? Also, when we danced together while I held your waist and wrapped around you to pull closer? Remember how our eyes were locked and lips were called for our first kiss? We made a promise in that balcony for our togetherness.

The outside world was complete silence for us. Because we were lost in each other's celebration. For the memories we felt ourselves younger; trust me, it was bliss for us to be called and remembered.

Yours everyday wakeup call was my favourite alarm and your goodbye hugs were my favourite place to be found. Like the silence in the tides of oceans are loud enough to be the calmest lullabies. But it is for those who understand and for the people in love. It is their love language to communicate.

Yes, in that balcony I still have a piece of my heart. But today after your cries and tears are tired to roll down your cheeks, please wipe yourself and wash your face to sing our favourite song at least for the one last time until my heart is heard. After you're done, I know you still remember our days. When the memories are rewinded, please don't forget to call me. I need to talk about thousands of things. When the music stops at your balcony, please find the missing piece of my heart that I have dropped. I am sure you would find it under your favourite pillow or inside your cosy blanket. Please return to me in the call and in between our conversation. Because I promise in that call, we both would cry and shed tears. Tears of emptiness and memories. Let's start our journey and let's walk holding hands in each other's life. Let us dance, and once again, I will wrap you in my arms to look at you. Let's lock our eyes and pull each other closer to feel each other's heartbeats. Let me whisper in your ears, 'I missed you' and unite ourselves with a kiss.

Don't let tomorrow happen with the lonely balcony. Let us decorate it with your favourite flowers and sweet scent of aroma to cheer and welcome the beautiful evening. Let us light the candle and call for the twining stars to curtain our twilight while we feel lost in each other's arms while cuddling each other.

I see my notepad at the edge of the table every time. My hand urges to reach; my heartbeat trembles to recall the old memories. My eyes will lose its sight. Yet, my footsteps reach to notepad, I began to write after my eleventh try.

Every time when this happens, I recall those days when my footsteps were getting closer and how I would reach it out. When this time I began writing, I am writing about my first love. Every first of my life. I say love is a magical journey; you slide over a rainbow in your life into those seven million colours, seven million emotions. Together we have lived, laughed and loved. When we slid our hands against those walls to make love, it was our first time.

Together we have kissed and unhooked to feed ourselves to love and lust. Like the ice sliding your back, it made my chin to go down and deeper to explode each other into the loudest moans, it was our first time.

Together we have roamed the city, danced in the middle of the streets at the midnight under the blanket of sparkling stars. We have boozed to lose the flaws in each other. We have hugged to our longing ecstasy while I whispered you to be my side forever, it was our first time.

But today, do you even observe how my texts are unseen and my calls are unanswered? Do you even recall how my hopes are shattered into pieces? Do you even know that I still choose to talk to you? Do you even know that I want to share all bits and pieces of my life with you even in my dreams? Because in those dreams, I see you every night. In those dreams, I want us to tangle once again around the scented aroma of fresh love.

Where did we ever lead to? And how did we ever start this? This life never allows you to step into yesterday nor can you jump forward to see where you would fall into. And today, I just took my notepad to write about you for the one last time.

I want to scream out from the bottom of my heart and until my throat is dried. To the unheard voices of mine, it never found a place to fly.

The deep besotted of me wandering off the million stars unhiding the melancholy. Ding-a-ling of the jingle bells, the snip snap whoosh of wood fire that makes me warm every time as a roaring blaze escaped in the dying branches of twigs before trembling into ashes.

The ash of me was never sacred because the memories of those still haunts me. Maybe I never stood infront of a mirror to see how tired this soul is, how much I have lost myself as an ambulatory in hide 'n' seek to understand what is mine. The sun sets and the dark appears, in the dusk those memories are faded. In my dreams, where I see her again. The petrichor of yesterday still makes me a lonely gaze. I wish I could drench in rain, the drops kissing my cheeks would tell me the void splattered inside me. The thunders of yesterday would say how badly I wanted you to stay. And those dark clouds remind me of every bad day. But the aroma of morning coffee makes me miss you even more with every sip.

After the rain, when my heart is still aching and my breathes are choking, I am here on the edge of the glory of the great fight of loving myself. The body is warm and jingles are never the same as I have heard before the rain yesterday. It's already dawn, everything is left as a memory.

Maybe I need to stand infront of the same mirror to make worth of my every try of which I had attempted to make you mine. Gazing at the million stars, I was just lost in my belief of you, 'you will be mine' which made my hide 'n' seek to stargaze when life was a like an ambulatory.

Loud little cries of a little beautiful soul were first heard on April 1999, my nine months of journey in my mother's womb gave me her glimpse of love and affection. The touch of her love to her sacrificing happiness to mine. I remember you adding sugar to the finely chopped tomatoes, which I otherwise refused to eat. The first painting of ours, adding colours to the big red heart, took me twenty-three tries to imperfectly match the masterpiece of yours. On the first day of my school when you dropped me walking a mile and I hugged you so hard before I stepped into the class.

Ssshhh, going back to the time, when I cried for the first time. There were the tears of joy and happiness filled the hall. I never had noticed that I was the reason. The two Kgs of flesh of mine had spread happiness across twenty million stars. I was carried from him to her, them to they and raised as the most blessed human being. I never realised in my twenty-four years of journey that you are my angel Mumma.

From the silent whispers of he is my son to the loudest prayers of save my son, the eternal powers of mystery were on my side. Yet again the hospital bed called me once again to hear my cries. I was neat to my last breath. The same hall of the hospital was filled with the tears of anguish and heartache. The same two Kgs of flesh of mine spread the prayers to reach twenty million goddesses. I could able to hear the voices consoling my Mumma.

I was just 75 days old, could hardly see the faces of the crowd. But I was sensing that I was safe in her arms. The whole world slept and swept to laughter and joy. But the world had left the little corner of the hospital bed to share our tears and prayers. This world had no idea about the sufferings of the two corned souls. I never realised in my twenty-four years of journey that you are my angel Mumma.

She started writing letters to her baby who was kicking her womb every now and then. The letters were filled with love, dreams, affection and the pride to see her son at the first glimpse. Every time it was flipped into a silent paper burn. But her thoughts haunted her every time. She saw me with the tears rolling down her eyes and that left me sacred by her last goodbyes.

This time, the whole world stood for us and gave a rhythm to our daily prayers. I was traumatised to believe that I am replying to their last goodbyes or will I be again carried into their hands to him to her; them to they. I never realised in my twenty-four years of journey that you are my angel Mumma.

Now, she started writing letters of her last touch, kisses, hugs and her bundle of love. And we both did not wanted to have our final goodbyes. My palm could barely lengthen to her pinky finger. Yet I loved to have a shake hand and not the goodbyes. And, when finally, the prayers were heard, I witnessed the tears of happiness filled the hall, I once again noticed that I was the reason for the celebration.

I have realised in my twenty-four years of journey that you are my only angel Mumma.

I have never cried for the love, because I never wanted to make it happen or to grab it as mine. But little I knew that love would happen when exactly it has to ring the bell. I knew love is a magic but I never knew that magic does not happen often.

I picture the rainbow, but I forget its beautiful colour like the colour in every rainbow portrays the beautiful events of love. I talk to the moon and stars but I forget that I was amidst the dark clouds.

I was drenched in rain waiting for you but I forget the lightning and thunders were louder than my voice to be heard for you.

In my balcony, I capture the reflection of the moon so beautifully to fall in love all over again, but in the same dark, I can even hear the echoes of the paper burn. I see you in the dark mist covering your beauty. Your footsteps arouse my sense, those curves wanders me in the heavens. In the dark under the million stars, I follow your footsteps with a heavy heart, my every silent footstep is a call for our love. Even the loudest of my cries were unheard. I remember your favourite cologne when I smell the rose in my corridor; Crossing my fingers, I take a peck to gaze the moon and whisper, 'Wish I was loved'.

Only my tears would understand the pain. I was lost and frightened, scared and terrified. Like every passing second, I felt there was so much happening around me. My little footsteps felt like a print of love on the seashore. For every wave hitting the shore, my footstep was being erased. But little more I cried for you to hold my hand in those hardships while enjoying the waves. Along with the wounds of loneliness, those memories of us spent together are my favourite lullaby. I still find every jingle boring without you, my side.

When I am no longer able to understand my own lyrics and when my songs are jumbled with its composition, trust me, I forgot the whole plot of my story while sipping the wine last night.

In those poems, I have written about the stars and their love, about the moon and its romance. But now, those jingles are not able to be heard anymore. There is a silence, the silence of my fears.

Once, when I was sitting in my balcony, my phone beeped to your notification, 'I miss you'. My eyes started to drop the tears of my love, tears of happiness. I switched off my cigar and packed my bag to start my bike to ride to you.

Your single message made me to hope in love and smile to feel the lost happiness. Now, I am there in your balcony by holding your hand. Your heart is racing, so is mine. I can feel your lips calling mine and my arms miss your hugs. We came closer, I put my hands on your waist, you caressed my hair and our lips were sealed to unlock the desires of love that we had missed.

After when the balcony has once again witnessed the aroma of love story and the scent has shared into our clothes, I can able to hear the forgotten jingles. I can soothe to my song; those lyrics are once again suiting perfectly to our story. I whisper my poem in your ears when those stars winked to our love, even the moon is shy to our romance. Little you understand that this night is young and our love is infinite.

~

You were silent when every time I wished to hear from you. Your voice makes me smile; your smile makes me dance in the cloud nine. Can you hold my hand for a little more while? While I brush the love that my heart talks about. To the dusk till the dawn, I will call you mine. Even the silence in my mime will talk of my love sign.

It's more than bursting myself with a heartbreak inside. I wish my love was conveyed. I know I failed. But you do understand that my love for you will never die. I don't say roses are red, violets are blue but rather I would say my voice is empty without you, my side.

I cannot take this silence anymore, because I have almost buried myself. I hope the ashes says how much I loved you every day. In those days, I felt myself hugged in your arms and cuddled while you stayed. But today, every wish has travelled until my grave. Oh, please at least talk to me now; I want to hear from you to tune my strings of a musical chord. I know even the radio in your backseat remembers our favourite song.

It's not only this much that I have to say, but it is beyond those stars that could sparkle in their own way. I can draw the rainbow but even its ends would never connect like our thoughts have never matched. And maybe that is the reason I wish you to hold my hand. But that's enough because my heart has talked much about love. But remember, you were silent every time when I wished to hear from you.

Hey, listen, how can I tell you and make you understand that this body is aching for your hugs and my heart is choking for your love? I had never thought this would be so difficult, but today, writing about you makes my hands shiver and I can hear my own heartbeat.

Sometimes I even feel like, am I living the mirage of my life or am I experiencing the things for real? But everything about you is just happening like magic. It is always the surprises, the excitement and the joy of happiness. I never had imagined that I would really write about you one day. But yeah, you got to believe in magic though.

When I saw you standing in your balcony, watching the horizon setting behind the mystic magnificent like creature, I saw the beautiful world just infront of me. Yes, it was you. It was you who was holding the coffee mug and singing the melodies while the birds flapped at you on their way home. I was just there and captured every moment that I felt was enough to be happy for a lifetime.

But yeah, when I stepped forward to hug you, it was then I realised that it was a mirage. But I couldn't convince myself to be standing alone without being wrapped in your arms. I wanted to feel home.

After when it is dark, you might feel the cool breeze and the chills of my memories. Please do not let it go. Because I remember that it was the winter when we made our first love. It was just two of us on the lost island, which for us felt like a dreamland. We had the perfect campfire that could steal a little cold and leave us just the memories. I remember the way we danced to the music which made us to look into each other's eyes, body was pulled closer to feel the warm breathes. I remember the way I wrapped my arms around your waist and the way you leaned forward to kiss me until later we realised, we had fallen in love. It was magic.

Of course, even after years, we are still together and together who are fallen in each other's arms. But this time, let us both climb the mountains and at the top, let's pitch ourselves a tent and make the barbeque with the nostalgic feel of a campfire. Let's sleep watching the horizon set behind the same mystic magnificent like creature. But this time, I will hug my beautiful world, not just like a mirage, but for real!

If you think this world is so great, do not forget it is also unfair. To the people you think are so kind-hearted, do not forget that are also simp-farted.

I say this because the universe has left me no hope and no moment to recollect as mine. To all the love and care; passion and dreams; destiny and desires; money and fame; success and people to call they are mine, I have lost everything. Everything except for a six feet land that buries me. But I am so happy and proud for 'I have given everything to the universe that has drowned me to an empty hand'.

At this hour, when I can hear only the cool breeze and feel the shivers on my skin, even my alcohol is unable to take the pain. I see the only star from my balcony and my cheeks kissed my tears. Eyes are speaking of her and of our love, of those moments, of those memories when we were together.

Last time when I was writing a poetry, my poetry spoke of our first meet, first hug, first date, first kiss and first romance to ours everything. But fate for me has changed. Today, it is so hard to believe that I have lost her. In my previous poetry, she was holding my palms and our fingers enclosed the gaps of each other. Even our eyes spoke of love.

With the racing heartbeat, the coffee mug on the table went unnoticed and our chairs in that café were never in our senses. It was a purely magical moment when she accepted my engagement ring. I was on cloud nine and so was her. That moment felt like it is truly ours and felt it would last forever.

Ours is a short love story. Not so fancy but we had kept it very romantic. I used to write poems for her and she used to sketch my candids. We never missed our morning coffees and goodnight hugs. Every day, we had a show of our little dramas, our personal diaries never read the imbalances of our love.

It was the morning of Christmas and she always loved celebrations. She always wanted to celebrate with me, be it anything. But later that night, I had to catch a flight for a business meet. I know that the day was dull and she cried in a corner. But I surprised her with an afternoon party for that Christmas. We both knew time was not sufficient to spend moments together because I was already up for the flight. We had our last hug and kisses before I left for the airport.

I was all set and excited about the business meet. I heard the voice, 'Welcome aboard'. My journey to the hotel went just like a flick. While checking into the hotel, my phone beeped to read, 'she is no more'. I was lost, blank, traumatised and was screaming aloud to burst myself into tears. Pain was loud and my heart was choking. I could not even believe if everything was happening for real. But I had to accept the fate.

My only ray of hope in life is now gone. The person who made me to believe in this universe is now just the only star. So, today my words on this paper are my memories of her and our love. 'All I had is now gone! All I have now is never mine'. Because today, every chapter of mine could find a conclusion is because of her. Unlike every poem of mine is the remembrance of her and our love.

Yes, I know that I cannot pen words beautifully. Beautifully to express myself and your love. But I believe poetry is not adding the fancy words in this fancy world. But I believe it is like the sweet sugary cupcake in every party and like a bliss of a rare diamond in every jewellery.

When you had told me that I write about sad, it was you who had told me that I was dull to shiver under the dark thunders. But you have forgotten that it was you who was standing beside without even hugging me to make me feel the warmth. It was all by myself standing aloof watching you forgetting me and fading away from my story of life.

On the other side, it was me who thought you would pull out an umbrella and protect me until you never noticed I was in love. I was hugging my shiver that was making me feel the numbness. Little you did not notice that I was out of cigars when my body needed the most while standing under the yellow street lights which hardly could be seen in the rain. I remembered the way your love that once hugged me to push away my every bad habits.

I wondered was it a blessing to have you on my side or my fate watching you fade away from the reach of my farthest eyesight. You left me without even trying to hug the love while I was shivering on the corner of the 18th street.

Now, I remember love is not material, we were strangers before we met in that late night club. The blue light beaming on your soft cheeks which looked like dumplings and those curves like an hourglass made my nerve chill. It was 11'o clock; I sipped my wine watching you in my first sight.

I remember that it was the first time I felt love in my life. Trust me I was back to sober in that party. All I waited was for your one looks at me to make this dreamer to feel that his dream has come true. And when I finally could take you to the same club on our first date, I was hit by the nostalgic emotion of trust and hope. For me, it was a dream come true when you accepted my love.

When I started writing about you and started twining our stories like a delicate bead. I was only feared of losing you, nothing else in the world was even a matter when I hoped you would be with me forever. Like the sun sets and the thick clouds appear before the storm, sorry, I didn't notice the heartful of pain in my next chapter. Yes, I could not able to read you nor your name; nor could feel your love in that chapter. It was then I understood this love is fading away.

But look at now, my hands are shivering to write about you and my choked heart cannot twine the beads like it did once. I am sorry I guess I need to accept about what you had told me. I do write about the sad. But little you understand I never plotted you to be my subject.

~

It's been quite a while since I've seen the purest clouds. The thunderstorms make me feel the best tunes of my life. Stringing to the moon and back, memories of us followed back. Like the pigeon flaps and dog wags, it reminds me of how our love has started.

It all started on my balcony. On the edge of my balcony, memories were created. Love was happened and before you were gone, I could still flavour the morning coffee. After which I saw the note written 'I love you', I witnessed the loudest thunderstorms and the dark clouds appeared with the million scars.

Little You Understand
That I am sitting in a corner, lost in your thoughts and wondering why it's been so long? Little do you understand, this world is crazy making you more lovely by leaving all the greys behind into the clumsy escapes. When I had planned to join the stars and table her around to cheer the wine, little she whispered, 'You are making this night unforgettable'.

Little You Understand
That I am busy loving you infinitely and calling for every bits of paper that could hold my secret love, my secret dreams that I once had cried for my love. When the stars

held my hand and sang a song, I realised that it was a knit of our endless talks. When our hearts fell in love, I wondered about the beautiful nights we made our love. All the glitters of our dreams where I am still lost in your memories just reminded me of those dark nights.

Little You Understand

Now, in my balcony, I am lonely just to see myself amidst the hoots of crying owls. Dogs are barking at the corner of this road and loneliness is echoing deep within me.

On the full moon day, how can I cry for the love, which is making my time feel darker? I wish it is raining here to make a paper boat and see how it sails through the direction.

Little You Understand

This balcony is calling for you, to hold the coffee mug and sing along with the chirps of the birds. The paper boat that I've sailed in the water, I wish to convey my love.

And now, I start to recollect why things were taking more time. Does the distance from me to reach my love to the stars was long for my paper boats? I was seized in time to wonder how love flies; it's been ages since I am calling you to cheer my wine glass and table with me forever.

Little You Understand

I am still writing my love letters to you until it reaches you. I will not stop making paper boats to sail until you understand I am still waiting for you in my balcony, holding my coffee mug.

Prateek S Kulkarni

www.ingramcontent.com/pod-product-compliance
Lightning Source LLC
LaVergne TN
LVHW061618070526
838199LV00078B/7325

9789356216808